PARSIVAL

PARSIVAL

Steve McCaffery

ROOF BOOKS
NEW YORK

ISBN: 978-1-93182-46-2
Library of Congress Control Number: 2015951882

 This book is made possible, in part, by the New York State Council on the Arts
with the support of Governor Andrew Cuomo and the New York State Legislature.

Roof Books
are published by
Segue Foundation
300 Bowery, New York, NY 10012
seguefoundation.com

Roof Books
are distributed by
Small Press Distribution
1341 Seventh Street
Berkeley, CA. 94710-1403
800-869-7553 or spdbooks.org

for a start try

      proofreading that

ELEGY written on

           a Tolkein mousepad

    it's an academical

way to

      fess up your

three-book membership

          points to

      what was it that

                mortuarized the CD

    Burner IN EFFIGY

      blue-tooth rap wrist

                  graphic *incident with*

            duo cheese tablet I'm

          that Mona Lisa flat

        panel monitor

              lizard alert patient

        and ethernetted on

          a table cloth—closest

     Turin shroud-print to

            ecclesiastical *history*

and iris-scan it

BURNS AND PLAYS

all my infrared alerts to

the tune of what if I think-pad

therefore am I an acrobat

with a yeast

inflexion Fluxus

Detroit or

London Fluxshoe

my joint is

out of time

what's yours?

World Wide

Wobble off

to Buffalo springs

sushi over

all the origami

Othello combos

FOR THE MASSES

that's not a

wheat crisis it's

A GENOCIDAL SHOWCASE

behind a shower

curtain no

problemo it

OPENS TO anyone

                    would seem to

        lower *the risk*

                                        of chronic

installation strangle

                                    it a little

            more *Dictatorship* of

                    the Propaedeutic all arms

        to THE INCINERATOR

turkey franks of

                    the world unite

you've only to put

                        those herbal collars on

            the Cardinals BEFORE

        they say MASS

                                    EXTERMINATION REACHES

    THE LAUNDRY BELT

                        detergent deterrent my

        ass up your nose

                            leave all *explanations*

        to Vesalius and

                        his merry men

    EVERY CENTURY'S

                    GONE AWAL LIP

            TENDERIZED MALLEABLE

                            MALEFICARUM GIVES

        your nipples a

sense of nappy

rash *brought* on at

18gb per second

CHANCE that's why

I call being *on*

Time now

salt up YOUR

wounds it's

TORTURERS appreciation

day at your

favorite Abu-

Starbucks either

"the cops came

blasting out" or

"Joyce learnt

another thing

from Anna Livia Plurabelle"

either

"you suddenly get

into a pause" or

else "you wish

you had it in

THE FIRST PLACE"

nothing but a

                              Smith &

              Weston Browning

                              ring *before the*

              book arrives puts

                                          a *nylon stocking*

                    on its face and

says it's

                              Marsilius of

        Padua *come*

                                    to rob the local

food bank

                          it's what some

                                          call an urban

                    gesture for the

          century

God

how awful   a radio

                              smells

            when it blows up

all those little bits of

                    toxic mass

                          blatter through the new

          invariance schemes

glad *I* lost *my* legs

as a boy IN

CELEBRITY CULTURE

it was a

Tutankhamen moment *in*

the mirror stage of

the Heisenberg principle

now I'm six legs better

and a friend of

local tadpoles

mapping magpies through

Cordelia plumage thanks

to *town planning*

according to

systematic   chance

generation

call me

"*Buddhist*"

if I talk TOO much

abnormally intelligent

chuckling facilitates

MY HEDGE FUND PLEBISCITES

with air

redirected from

the Xerox

ducts

downtown

where

everyone thinks

the word

"gay" is

a four-letter word for

"queer"

IMPORTED FROM

THE MEYKONG

DELTA

edition of

Seneca's treatise

On

Clemency such

antinomianism

gives provocative

challenge a

bad name

but at

least it's

a name not

a number

LOST IN

THE LATEST

Darfur STATISTICS

globalize

so Mothers of

the Nation can

live overseas

clean

their teeth in

the Ganges

version of

TEXT-MESSAGING

while making love

in a concept

of oblique

distrust

THE IMPACT OF

a vertical pin-prick

being equal to

a shot-gun wedding to

an androgynous girl

named Valent**o   knowing

the heroin

route trails

right into his/ her

wallet where

it MASQUERADES as

a Communist lodger named

          Mrs. O'Malley

she's learning

   nano *technology*

      IN order to

            hypnotize TSUNAMIS

part of

      the never ending

  five year plan   of

        being WASHED

     UP forgotten

 and unmourned

            domestically

A few yards

      FROM a Law Library

  some Heavenly City

     reappears

          its suburbs

    quivering

in ellipses around

        A CENTER WHICH

    DOES NOT

coincide *with*

                                       the latest

shopping-mall as

                     an *interactive*

learning environment

all *physicists*

                  are prejudiced

by contrast

                      some neonate

mammals

        are plastic *and*

OPEN and

       love *spicy*

            food

compared TO

                         sociology

the nuptial flight

           of the hermit bat

is quite grandiose

      drawing FIRST

BLOOD from

                 the barricades

set up by

cybernetics in the 1950s

that allowed all this

in THE

first place

LEPROSY   then Interpol

on a World

Map depicts

a **GOD** with

the mind OF

a mathematician

NURTURED on

PREDICAMENTS in

mail-order

real estate

and fossil farming

to inverse

tractor poaching

suckled at

the template

of more

sensory

depravations but

who's complaining

socially programmed

to bungee jumping

into fuel conservation

and continental

breakfasts with

THE POPE

sequoias and wolves

subscribe to

the *challenge* OF

LIBERALISM STILL BUYING

female portraits

OF *the*

latest in

SADO-MASOCHISTIC

cartels

speech melodies

burst with

ANECDOTES but still

lack *full*

frontal paranoia

AMONG FRIENDS

IN THE

KNOWLEDGE INDUSTRY

THAT SAID the

possibility of

record linkages

via comparative

database analyses

allows your

mind to be

genetically anybody

else's

when

IT'S HAPPY HOUR ALL DAY

in Ancient

Wisdom *where*

nothing's happening

to Homer's

gin and tonic

MIXED WITH

Sappho's lentil

soup

as

two gorillas

with AIDS

form

a SUICIDE

pact using

NOM-DE-PLUMES

to *enter*

the meat-processing

system with

a final kiss

before

canning

relax

they're now part

of the

Club World™

menu with

parsley enzyme

instead of

coriander FOR

garnish

WHENEVER

sea and land

is POLITICS

points towards

the stellar criterion

of   *metanoia* — theory's

                           Berlin wall

kiss it *with*

        wet lips

            the political

promise always

          THE man

       of the

           INCH BY INCH

potestas   *potentia*

              Senator Amphibrach Jr.

out of his

       FRACTAL FASCISM

             the new

dawn TO

       END dawns

    allons enfants

            de la

    patrie for

                my heart

aches and A

       drowsy numbness

pains my

SENSE BROUGHT

INTO contrast

with a person from

Porlock

like me

who is

no less in

person than

is you

when immersed

in all

known instruments

of UTTERANCE

utterance that is

AS SIGNIFICATORY

EXPULSION COME

TO DWELL

IN THE ACT

OF writing   where

we wandered

lonely as

clouds in that

Romantic

COMMUNITY

ATTESTED AND

  recollected

                    in tranquility

                                            THE SAME

              slings and

                            arrows of

OUTRAGEOUS shot

                                          through any

              number of

        PERCEPTUAL IMPLICATIONS

                              no allegory

              this is

                                                    OF the middle

                    disposition

trans evangelized by

                                        weekend television

              though the therapy

                                          is tangible

              in its rolling

                              "ths"   broad

              instigations   are   all   that's

        left

                        of *the wild*

seduction

the bald   soprano

expresses THIS   *by way*

of the   FLUID   radius

attached

yet incomplete

in

its

SIDEREAL

PAUSE

recovery of   the true

Aristotle   MEANING   there are slaves

BY   NATURE   bring them

to Rome   across   A   short

TEAR IN   THE flow-chart   POLITICA-REPUBLICA

and we'll   settle

the   score

       alternatively   write

       a poem

IN WHICH

       each

word   is

TO

a   source   in

a   corresponding   citational

traced

REFERENCE   e.g.

"Each

Saturday   arrives

on *foot*"   *becomes*

line   3

rd
3rd

                              word   p.

        169   G.   F.

                        W.

              Hegel   *Lectures*

    on   etc.   it's

              either   a

                                              language game

            or

                                              the poncho

  interim   across

                    a   festooned

  gradient   ditto   a

                              brilliance

now

the   *fuckwinds*

are

fledged

each   serafin

efficacy

squandered   cromlechs   in

rock   basins   charge *the*

Cassivellanus   *specimens*

FIGURES   pierce

THE PRECIPITATE

flight

they *have*   *all*

the

qualities   John

Brown   attributed

                    to   Keswick

                        beauty

HORROR   and   immensity
        ·

        meeting   Godot   and   leaving

him   BEHIND   as

        THE   SILENCE   *of an*   *axiom*

IN the

pulsating   circle of   YOU KNOW what or

            perhaps   AS

        the   ombudsman   of   TRUTH

STILL   I

                            like   *your*

patience

part

Chartist   *at the*

thought   of

liberation   and   *sex*

being   alone

the

PARADOXICAL

roulette   a

Jesuit

from

outer

space sounds

a little

too

Romantic or

PERHAPS

an ELSEWHERE

isn't

such

an   ordinary

space

skillfully   seductive

BEHIND

appearances

it's   *the night* of

THE "tidy"

MAN IN RAGS

hardly

a suddenncss

to jump from

a name

placed over

A FACE of

an eyelash

AT

MIDNIGHT   let's

say in the

                                             risk   of

                          LOSING it

                     to   appendectomy

a

                holding

                                pattern

     to

              the   *new*

             articulation

                      hair

   bent on

a claw's

nose-attila

kissed   from a

bias   portal stimulant

conceptual gaps merge

to new   flange arbiters

sorry to say

that

tickles   up

THE hoopla stage

of

CRUMBLING

fissure

FISCAL *tilt from*

prime

to

camber PRIVILEGE

and all

FOR A try

at

politics

sad

haloed Hades

in some notes

just

a

bias

toward

non-sesame casino

SOLIPSISM

over

SUN-KISSED

crenellations none

WHERE

CHANCE might be

the tenderness

AROUND

diploma

throat-flaneurs

our

literality not A

LIFE-TIME

exemplar

across Kantian kilt

BACK TO FRONT

brushed

to *a safe*

house

cocaines the

CRACKS

gathers spunk-head

STABILITIES

as two

fingers pop

a sputnik

on her arm

chuffed

breeze through

THE   follicle

GRID

as arm &

army

PRISONS

act

A pact in

CONCENTRATED camps

the syllables

emit

their vomit-

furniture elopes

the slope

turns out

to be

a DEATH squad's beards

THE SEVERED

ARM

negotiates

with beetles

swarming

a throttled

passport

gens

sans papiers

an electric

fan

PROTECTS

the toothbrush

from

illegal teeth

THE frown

        smiles

         pastoral

             erases

   epic

          SPACE

    "HE PLACES" IN

A GAMBIT-DANCE

            beside

      shawls frumity

THEN

PROCEEDS

ALONG

a titulan

gives script

ALONG the way

TO soup

anomalies

while

the dead in

MASS GRAVES

are

ceremoniously

baptized

with numbers:

Arras

UNKNOWN Man

5

who

urged

THAT

the PHILOSOPHY

OF consciousness

be replaced

WITH

THE dialectic of

CONCEPT

MATTERS it

by haps

a camera

is not

a camera   without

the box

it

comes in

torn

ragged

spaces REACHED

BY MACHINES

HELD TOGETHER

in paper

clipped

proceduralities

throws theory

to a burning house

as prose

ABJECT

OBJECT

seems

apart

improbable

coincident anxiety

brought on

BY

a DISCARDED

convention

SHALL WE GO IN ?

the two of us

                                as

                                              a collective shadow

                         of

                           some hedge-fund

                                    speculation

                                  even

                                        old-

            testament

            prophets

                                are

                flocking to

                Micro

soft

porn

PESPIRATION

DRIPS

INTO

A toilet

bowl

or other

styles

of readymade

with

an

edifying

Oedipus

TOPOGRAPHY

as

HIGH

FIDELITY in

Castrol

which

Lieutenant

Lou

last saw

in action at

Saipan

IGNITES

TWO KITTENS

FROM

a

primary

source

OF inflammation

on

the papaya

badly

chipped

HIS OWN

SCREAM-WARRANTY

UNCERTAIN

by

known

distribution

PROTOCOLS

of hints

from

tabloids   to

Majolica

PROFILES

DEIFIED

IN

Aztec

SYMMETRY

CUT

LOOSE

the raft

for Pike's

Peak

seven

at an estimate

a

cabinet-

maker's

dictionary

replaces

marble sites

for *delivery*

to WHERE

the tapestries

DECODED IN

THE LIGHT

foxing

FROM *some*

Riviera

MAPS

span

eight

centuries of

damage

Hardyesque &

known

throughout the *plasma routes*

in

ISOLATE

Hudibras

claims each

sewn

in PAPER

GONDOLAS

TO EASE

THE crease

in

THE

TECTONIC

PLATES

FROM

AUTHORS

OF

A SET OF

twenty

wooden

cubes

arranged

in *polyglot*

CHRONOLOGIES

the metals

                              polished

                         in

          High

                                                        Dutch

                    a book

                                   of food

BROWNED

BY

RECRUITING

members in

THE IMAGINARY

diary

of A WIFE

FOUND

competent

TO

NAVIGATE

THE

incorrections

IN

four

volumes

of cement

or similar

accessories

to MURDER

all

armorial

spotting on

A LANDLORD'S

pencil

RUSTBELT

scimitar

FORMS

CHIPPED

from two

LETTER

S

WRITTEN on

a

different

day

`

imploded

by

A METROPOLIS

of *body*

parts

late Spring

TO   a

watchman's

clock

                                        half

        distance from

                                        the goal line

        THAT

                        too plain

                                                EVIDENCE

OF

other

recollections

among

Roman

ruins

in

THE year

of

7

Jaguar

Channel change

from INSTRUCTIONS

in a kidney cell

fuck   *the ethics*

of

stock   piles

she's putting all her money in

Iranian

enriched

uranium

developments

it's now

manufactured by

Baskin

but

Robbins   as *a*

mystery flavor

in a

HIDDEN

Tehran *latrine complex*

helping

ecopoetics copulate

with some

vegetable based

détant

WHOSE

SOLE

EXPRESSION IS

THE WORKING CLASS

I'm sure

the Cro-Magnon

                                        didn't have

                A NAME FOR it

THAT neat central

                                    REARRANGEMENT for

                    next time's cut-off number to

the algebraic possibilities

        the symphonic VARIANT

            seems lacustrine .

                    distributes

its opportunity

for limit fade

DRESSED in you AS YOURS

if

the funeral channel *teaches*

IN

a skinned face

about

THE shoulder slang

BREATHE DEEP   take

the lung's

                cyanogens

                        AS

                                                screen

COMPOSITE

                                                rescinds

                                                its

                cuckoo

JUVENILIA

so

EXIT

Goofy

ENTER

Minnie

Mouse

via

an allophonic

jolt

rogue

operatives

in

THAT *Acapulco*

PALPITANT

SHARD

TO A CRISIS

equivalent

to

"fuck

off"

not

long ago

themselves

ammunition

for

the speaker

talking

twenty

meters

to

THE MINUTE

from

the point

of impact

at

THE REST

of time

in *which*

you say

your

cough

has

LEFT YOU

a place in

THE CENTRAL

discount PARTURITION

frost robins congregate

slouch – salmon in

SOMETHING a car might hesitate

across

the device

ATTEMPTED fusion

WHICH *someone forgets* suggests

"*sanity*

and

ensemble"

sparks

mental alert to

the rigmarole

(sandwich

gone

which BROUGHT us there

TO day NOT date)

IMPOSSIBLE portents

pertinence

elsewhere

THE infomercial

codifies

the carbon nano tubes

IN QUORUM sensation

a turbine string

feeds its polytypal OCCULTATION

closelier mostly

a ghost for A PAST

last listing OF

the *energy* tradition

PLAGUE microbes conjugate

in LATENT DICTATORSHIPS to

form

a mediality *without ends*

enclitic attention AGHAST

at ripe crypts STRIPPED

azimuth of coral at

THE PLANKTON depth

of a horse hoof sidles in

the BRAIN-thought nutrient urge to

an off-shore TUMULT near parity

puts all a little west of

the eczema extension

skin slit and

the warren INACTIVE

genetic

navigation patterns

traffic JAMS

à la mode

falsify

the donor FATIGUE among

client *refugees*

a bard spits then *sings*

Jihadist websites link   UP TO

all relevant quotations

"since there's no soap come

let us piss and fart"

cold weather spokesmen of

the inclement balance

shadow recalls

DEPARTURE OF a face

ambivalent

to smiling

a fetish sphinx SNAPS in synapse

pulse trails reflecting from ITS iron column

in variant echo STRENGTHS

a series down

the Fresnel PATTERNS STILL HOLDING

to complete THE ENDING

yourself

ROOF BOOKS
the best in language since 1976

Recent & Selected Titles

• The Photoggrapher by Ariel Goldberg. 84 p. $15.95

• antisocial patience by David Brazil. 122 p. $15.95

• TOP 40 by Brandon Brown. 138 p. $15.95

• DEAD LETTER by Jocelyn Saidenberg. 98 p. $15.95

• THE MEDEAD by Fiona Templeton. 314 p. $19.95

• LYRIC SEXOLOGY VOL. 1 by Trish Salah. 138 p. $15.95

• INSTANT CLASSIC by erica kaufman 90 p. $14.95

• A MAMMAL OF STYLE by Kit Robinson
& Ted Greenwald. 96 p. $14.95

• VILE LILT by Nada Gordon. 114 p. $14.95

• DEAR ALL by Michael Gottlieb. 94 p. $14.95

• FLOWERING MALL by Brandon Brown. 112 p. $14.95.

• MOTES by Craig Dworkin. 88 p. $14.95

• APOCALYPSO by Evelyn Reilly. 112 p. $14.95

• BOTH POEMS by Anne Tardos. 112 p. $14.95

Roof Books are published by
Segue Foundation
300 Bowery • New York, NY 10012
For a complete list,
please visit roofbooks.com

Roof Books are distributed by
SMALL PRESS DISTRIBUTION
1341 Seventh Street • Berkeley, CA. 94710-1403.
spdbooks.org